A CELEBRATION
OF MOTHERS

A CELEBRATION OF MOTHERS

A Keepsake Devotional Featuring the
Inspirational Verse of Helen Steiner Rice

BARBOUR
PUBLISHING

ISBN 978-1-60260-299-1

The poetry of Helen Steiner Rice is published under a licensing agreement with the Helen Steiner Rice Foundation.

Special thanks to Virginia J. Ruehlmann for her cooperation and assistance in the development of this book.

Devotional writings originally published in *Daily Wisdom for Mothers* by Michelle Medlock Adams and *Just Call Me Mom*, both published by Barbour Publishing, Inc.

Scripture quotations marked KJV are taken from the King James Version of the Bible.

Scripture quotations marked NIV are taken from the HOLY BIBLE, NEW INTERNATIONAL VERSION®. NIV®. Copyright © 1973, 1978, 1984 by International Bible Society. Used by permission of Zondervan. All rights reserved.

Scripture quotations marked NLT are taken from the *Holy Bible*, New Living Translation, copyright © 1996, 2004. Used by permission of Tyndale House Publishers, Inc. Wheaton, Illinois 60189, U.S.A. All rights reserved.

Scripture quotations marked MSG are from *THE MESSAGE*. Copyright © by Eugene H. Peterson 1993, 1994, 1995, 1996, 2000, 2001, 2002. Used by permission of NavPress Publishing Group.

Scripture quotations marked NASB are taken from the New American Standard Bible, © 1960, 1962, 1963, 1968, 1971, 1972, 1973, 1975, 1977, 1995 by The Lockman Foundation. Used by permission.

Scripture quotations marked NKJV are taken from the New King James Version®. Copyright © 1982 by Thomas Nelson, Inc. Used by permission. All rights reserved.

Cover and interior illustration: Todd Williams

Published by Barbour Publishing, Inc., P.O. Box 719, Uhrichsville, Ohio 44683, www.barbourbooks.com

Our mission is to publish and distribute inspirational products offering exceptional value and biblical encouragement to the masses.

Member of the
Evangelical Christian
Publishers Association

Printed in China.

Contents

A MOTHER'S HOPE

A MOTHER'S BLESSING

A Celebration of Mothers

What joy there is in being a mother! We are blessed with little lives to have and hold, to nurture and love, to protect and cherish. What an awesome challenge! What a wonderful opportunity! What a blessing from the Lord!

From the day we hold our children in our arms, we are awestruck by the sight of ten tiny fingers, ten tiny toes, and the innocent, loving eyes of the miracles that God has wrought. And we are forever changed.

As each day passes, we watch our children grow. Soon they are walking and talking. And before we know it, we're sending them off to kindergarten. Then, after struggling through the adolescent years, they are graduating from school, leaving our nest, beginning new lives, and starting the cycle of life all over again as they form new families of their own.

And we are left with the memories of what seems like just yesterday, when we held them in our arms, counted their ten tiny fingers and their ten tiny toes, felt their baby breath upon our necks, and reveled in their soft grunts and groans, sighs and cries, wiles and smiles.

As you read the poems, devotionals, and prayers within the pages that follow, allow God to fill your heart, mind, and spirit with hope and love as you celebrate your life as a mother, today and every day, through the good times and bad. Take strength from your Daddy God, who, like us, has no greater love than of that for His children. And rejoice in this *Celebration of Mothers*!

A MOTHER'S HEART

*The heart of a mother is a deep abyss at the bottom
of which you will always find forgiveness.*

HONORÉ DE BALZAC

Be an example. . .in what you say,
in the way you live,
in your love,
your faith,
and your purity.

1 TIMOTHY 4:12 NLT

MOTHERHOOD

The dearest gifts that heaven holds,
the very finest, too,
Were made into one pattern
that was perfect, sweet, and true.
The angels smiled, well pleased, and said,
"Compared to all the others,
This pattern is so wonderful
let's use it just for mothers!"
And through the years, a mother has
been all that's sweet and good,
For there's a bit of God and love
in all true motherhood.

~HSR

The Motherhood Journey

Every good gift and every perfect gift is from above, and comes down from the Father of lights, with whom there is no variation or shadow of turning.

JAMES 1:17 NKJV

*H*ave you ever heard the expression, "Be happy where you are on the way to where you're going"? If you're always looking to the future with longing, you'll miss the good stuff going on right now. You have to find the right balance.

My daughters do this from time to time. When they were younger, they'd get so many presents for Christmas that they couldn't enjoy the ones they'd already opened because they were so focused on opening the next gift. They would hardly look at the roller skates they'd just received before they were on to the next package. It wasn't until all of the presents were unwrapped that they could actually enjoy the blessing load they'd been given.

Have you been guilty of that, too? Are you looking for the next present to unwrap instead of enjoying the blessing load all around you? It's easy to do—especially if you're in the diaper, teething, can't-get-back-into-your-prepregnancy-clothes stage. Some days it's hard to find the "gift" in all of it, but look closely. There are gifts all around. Enjoy this wonderful motherhood journey. Don't miss a minute of it. Every moment should be treasured. You have to enjoy today before you'll ever really appreciate tomorrow.

WHAT IS A MOTHER?

It takes a mother's love to make a house a home—
A place to be remembered no matter where we roam.
It takes a mother's patience to bring a child up right
And her courage and her cheerfulness to
make a dark day bright.
It takes a mother's thoughtfulness to
mend the heart's deep hurts
And her skill and her endurance to
mend little socks and shirts.
It takes a mother's kindness to forgive us when we err,
To sympathize in trouble and to bow her head in prayer.
It takes a mother's wisdom to recognize our needs
And to give us reassurance by her loving words and deeds.

~HSR

My Mother

Do not exasperate your children; instead,
bring them up in the training and instruction of the Lord.
Ephesians 6:4 niv

*I*f my mother had been a different woman, I would be a different person. When she read to me each night, I learned about the world of words; today I make my living writing—and I still love coming home from the library with a stack of books to keep me company.

When my mother took me outdoors and named the trees and flowers and birds for me, I learned about the world of nature. Today, whenever I'm upset or discouraged, I still find peace, walking in the woods; and when I recognize ash and beech, trilliums and hepatica, purple finches and indigo buntings, I feel as though I'm saying the names of dear, old friends.

And when my mother prayed with me each night and before each meal, I learned about an eternal world; today I seek God's presence daily and offer up my life to Him in prayer.

My mother trained me well.

MOTHER IS A WORD CALLED LOVE

Mother is a word called love,
And all the world is mindful of
The love that's given and shown to others
Is different from the love of mothers. . .
For mothers play the leading roles
In giving birth to little souls—
For though small souls are heaven-sent
And we realize they're only lent,
It takes a mother's loving hands
And her gentle heart that understands
To mold and shape this little life
And shelter it from storm and strife. . .
No other love than mother love
Could do the things required of
The one to whom God gives the keeping
Of His wee lambs, awake or sleeping. . .
So mothers are a special race
God sent to earth to take His place,
And "Mother" is a lovely name
That even saints are proud to claim.

~HSR

Our Children

These commandments that I give you today are to be upon your hearts.
Impress them on your children. Talk about them when you sit at home and
when you walk along the road, when you lie down and when you get up.
Tie them as symbols on your hands and bind them on your foreheads.
Write them on the doorframes of your houses and on your gates.
Deuteronomy 6:6–9 niv

The house rumbles with laughter and tussles. I hurry to keep up with it all. They are a heritage that comes from You. These bursts of energy in various sizes and personalities are like arrows in a warrior's hands.

I call on You for wisdom. Each day I thank You for guidance in handling different situations. Thank You, Lord, for how You help me teach our children about Your love. I treasure Your leading as I share Your lessons with them while we go about our activities at home, when we share walks, as we pray together at bedtime, and rise each morning to face a new day.

My husband and I have dedicated our lives and these children to You, Lord. I know for sure Your hand is and will be upon them throughout their entire lives.

I write Your words on plaques, pictures, and on our doorposts that, "'As for me and my household, we will serve the Lord'" (Joshua 24:15 niv).

MOTHERS ARE SPECIAL PEOPLE

Mothers are special people
In a million different ways,
And merit loving compliments
And many words of praise,
For a mother's aspiration
Is for her family's success,
To make the family proud of her
And bring them happiness. . .
And like our heavenly Father,
She's a patient, loving guide,
Someone we can count on
To be always on our side.

~HSR

BELIEVING THE BEST

[Love] always protects, always trusts, always hopes, always perseveres.
1 CORINTHIANS 13:7 NIV

Recently, our pastor preached a sermon I'll not soon forget. His topic? Love. I've heard hundreds of sermons about love, but I'd never heard it preached quite like this. He said, "Love always believes the best in others."

Yikes! Just when I thought my love walk was shaping up, he zapped me! I wrote it down this way in my journal: "Love always believes the best—especially in my children."

It's a tough world out there and getting tougher all the time. Our children are faced with many challenges. Sometimes, we're the only ones believing the best in them. We're the only ones cheering them on to victory. We're the only ones making them feel special. Sometimes, we're the only ones on their side.

Believing the best in our children doesn't mean turning our heads when they act inappropriately. Rather, it means giving them the benefit of the doubt. If they say they turned in their homework and yet you receive a note that says they didn't, you believe them, assuming the teacher has misplaced it. Then, pray with your child that the teacher will find the missing homework. You know, if we believe the best in our children, we'll get the best from our children.

MOTHER

Whose hands bestow more fragrant bouquets
Than Mother, who daily speaks kind words of praise—
Mother, whose courage and comfort and cheer
Light bright little candles in hearts through the year.
No wonder the hands of an unselfish mother
Are symbols of sweetness unlike any other.

~HSR

THAT ENCOURAGING SPIRIT

Gently encourage the stragglers, and reach out for the exhausted, pulling them to their feet. Be patient with each person, attentive to individual needs.

1 THESSALONIANS 5:14 MSG

When I was a college cheerleader, we did the whole, "Give me a G! Give me an O!" You get the idea. Yes, that was "a few" years ago, and my cheerleading uniform is faded and in storage, but that encouraging spirit still remains. I'm still the resident cheerleader of our house. That's what moms do, right? Don't you feel like a cheerleader most of the time?

Our children (and our spouses, too!) need our encouragement. They need to hear us say, "You can do it!" They need to hear us say, "You have got it going on!" They need our support and unconditional love on a daily basis. Of course, we cheerleaders need encouragement, too. In order to have encouragement to dish out, we have to fill ourselves up again. We do that by praising the Lord, praying to God, reading His Word, and taking care of ourselves by getting enough rest. Don't let yourself get empty and rundown or you'll be the grouchiest cheerleader in the history of the sport! Now, go forth and "Give me a GO! GO! GO!"

A MOTHER'S LOVE

A mother's love is something that no one can explain—
It is made of deep devotion and of sacrifice and pain.
It is endless and unselfish and enduring, come what may,
For nothing can destroy it or take that love away.
It is patient and forgiving when all others are forsaking,
And it never fails or falters even though the heart is breaking.
It believes beyond believing when the world around condemns,
And it glows with all the beauty of the rarest, brightest gems.
It is far beyond defining, it defies all explanation,
And it still remains a secret like the mysteries of creation—
A many-splendored miracle man cannot understand
And another wondrous evidence of God's tender,
guiding hand.

~HSR

Love Is the Answer

Love one another deeply, from the heart.
1 Peter 1:22 NIV

"Mommy, will you always love me?" Abby asked, looking up at me with her big green eyes.

"Of course, I'll always love you," I said, kissing her on the head. "That's what mommies do."

Abby smiled, satisfied with my answer.

At that moment, I thought, *I hope she will always be able to feel my love—no matter what. Or, if she can't feel my love, I want her to feel God's love. His love is much more far-reaching than mine.*

Today's world is very unsure. In fact, it's crazy many days. In the hustle and bustle of day-to-day life, our children need our affirmation. They need to know that we'll always love them. And more importantly, they need to know that their heavenly Father will always love them. So, take this opportunity to tell them that you love them and that God loves them even more than you do—and that's a lot!

Love is the answer. Even if your children wander from "the straight and narrow path," love will bring them back. If you're discouraged today because your children don't seem to be accepting your love or embracing God's love—hold on! God's love has a way of penetrating even the hardest of hearts.

WHERE THERE IS LOVE

Where there is love the heart is light,
Where there is love the day is bright.
Where there is love there is a song
To help when things are going wrong.
Where there is love there is a smile
To make all things seem more worthwhile.
Where there is love there's a quiet peace—
A tranquil place where turmoils cease.
Love changes darkness into light
And makes the heart take wingless flight.
And mothers have a special way
Of filling homes with love each day,
And when the home is filled with love,
You'll always find God spoken of,
And when a family prays together
That family also stays together.
And once again a mother's touch
Can mold and shape and do so much
To make this world a better place
For every color, creed, and race.

~HSR

Reflected Love

"By this all men will know that you are my disciples, if you love one another."
John 13:35 NIV

*B*ecause God's love is reflected in ours, our children will learn about God simply through motherhood's love. Oh, we need to teach our children about God and His Word. We need to read them Bible stories and pray with them, answer their questions, and take them to church. We need to live in such a way that they'll see what it means to be a Christian. But on a much more basic level, they'll understand about a God who always hears, because when they were babies we responded to their cries. They'll be able to have faith in a God who meets their needs, because we saw that they never went hungry. God's strength and tenderness will be real to them because they caught a glimpse of it in our love, from the time they were born.

So, mothers, never let the world tell you that what you do is not important. Remember, when you rock your babies and sing a lullaby, your arms and voice are God's. When you do load after load of dirty diapers, and then grass-stained play clothes, and finally school clothes smeared with ketchup and chocolate pudding, remember, your hands are God's hands. And when you love your children unconditionally, all the way from colic to adolescent rebellion, you are loving with God's love. Through you, He will imprint Himself on your children's hearts.

Dear Lord,
Thank You for blessing me with children. May I be someone they can count
on each and every day, encouraging them as they grow up in Your light.
Hear these words of my heart—my God, my Father, my Friend. Amen.

A MOTHER'S JOY

*The art of mothering is handed down
from one generation to the next.*
WENDY JEAN RUHL

*The joy of the L*ORD *is your strength.*

NEHEMIAH 8:10 KJV

Meet the Success Family

Would you like an introduction to the family of Success?. . .
Well, meet the father—he is Work. The mother is Ambition.
The children are a source of pride—
they uphold the best tradition.
The oldest son is Common Sense, Perseverance is his brother,
While Honesty and Foresight are twins to one another.
The daughter's name is Character,
her sisters' names are Cheer
And Loyalty and Courtesy and Purpose That's Sincere.
The baby of the family is mighty sweet to know.
Her name is Opportunity; you'll want to see her grow.
And if you get acquainted with the father, you will find
The members of his family are just the nicest kind,
And if you form a friendship with the family of Success,
You'll get an introduction to a house of happiness.

~HSR

THE ROAD TO SUCCESS AND HAPPINESS

Come, children, listen closely;
I'll give you a lesson in GOD worship.
PSALM 34:11 MSG

*I*f you could teach your children only ten things before you died, what would you share? Would you teach them to stand up for who they are in Christ Jesus? Would you teach them self-defense? Would you teach them good manners? Would you teach them to give to others? Would you teach them to treat others with respect? Would you teach them how to be a friend?

It's a tough call, isn't it? There are so many things we want to impart to our kids. We want to save them from making all of the stupid mistakes that we made. While we can't protect them from every mistake, we can put them on the road to success and happiness.

We can make the most of every opportunity to teach them about the nature of God—God the Healer, God the Provider, God the Savior, God the Deliverer, God the Great I Am! There are chances every day to share little lessons with our children. Ask the Lord to help you identify those opportunities so that you can take advantage of each one.

BABY

A wee bit of heaven drifted down from above—
A handful of happiness, a heart full of love.
The mystery of life so sacred and sweet,
The giver of joy so deep and complete.
Precious and priceless, so loveable, too—
The world's sweetest miracle, baby, is you.

~HSR

THE GIFT OF MOTHERHOOD

From birth I have relied on you; you brought me forth from my mother's womb.
I will ever praise you.
PSALM 71:6 NIV

You would think that this was my first pregnancy, not my fourth; I am filled with such a sense of excitement and anticipation. Everything feels so new. Every kick and prod, every roll and tumble that this child delivers, fills me with awe. I am consumed with the yearning to hold and cuddle, to nurture, to bring this little person into a family eagerly awaiting the opportunity to love someone new.

Even with three more months of waiting, I am almost obsessed with thoughts of being ready. I am absurdly giddy over recent purchases—bottles, burp cloths, diapers. Friends watch and smile and shake their heads. "She's done all this before, what's the big deal?"

I'm not quite sure. Maybe I'm cherishing this experience so much because I know the pain of losing a life. Maybe it's the realization that I'm not getting any younger, and this may be our last child.

Whatever the reason, through it all—the discomfort, the nausea, the sickness, the aches and pains—I am always aware of the miracle growing within me. I praise my Creator for the gift of motherhood—and for the privilege and honor of serving Him in this way.

HEART GIFTS
FROM MOTHER

It's not the things that can be bought
that are life's richest treasures—
It's just the little "heart gifts" that money cannot measure.
A cheerful smile, a friendly word, a sympathetic nod
Are priceless little treasures from the storehouse of our God.
They are the things that can't be bought with
silver or with gold,
For thoughtfulness and kindness and love are never sold.
They are the priceless things in life for which no one can pay,
And the giver finds rich recompense in giving them away.
And who on earth gives more away and does
more good for others
Than understanding, kind and wise and selfless,
loving mothers,
Who ask no more than just the joy of helping those they love
To find in life the happiness that they are dreaming of.

~HSR

What Love Means

[Love] is not self-seeking.
1 CORINTHIANS 13:5 NIV

*L*ove means putting others' needs and desires before your own. Of course, as moms, we are well aware of that fact. When my girls were toddlers, they had many needs and desires. In fact, it seemed that one of them needed something from me all the time. If I had taken a shower by 3 p.m., I was doing well.

Especially when our children are little, we get to learn firsthand that aspect of love. And, some days, it's not easy. There were times when I prayed, "Please, God, just let them nap at the same time today so I can take a long, hot bath." (Hey, I would've paid a thousa dollars for a bubble bath back then!) Those were precious times, boy, they were busy times, too!

Maybe you're living those busy days right now. Maybe you're reading this and thinking, *Precious days? I want to escape!* Well, despair. God cares about your crazy, busy days. He knows that th "mom gig" isn't an easy job. He wants to give you rest and peace, He is well pleased with your well doing. So, the next time you hea "Mommy!" and you want to run the other direction—take heart! Yo are growing in love.

MOTHER PUTS THE
JOY IN EVERY DAY

Who puts the joy in every day?
Who makes it glad in every way?
Who knows the nicest things to say?
It's Mother!
Who understands and always hears?
Who helps us dry our falling tears?
Who just grows sweeter with the years?
It's Mother!
Who is our helper and our guide?
Who always looks on us with pride?
Who's always there whate'er betide?
It's Mother!

~HSR

If You Want Joy

Thou wilt shew me the path of life: in thy presence is fulness of joy;
at thy right hand there are pleasures for evermore.
Psalm 16:11 kjv

Just as the simple presence of the mother makes the child's joy, so does the simple fact of God's presence make our joy. The mother may not make a single promise to the child, nor explain any of her plans or purposes, but she is, and that is enough for the child. And to the child, there is behind all that changes and can change the one unchangeable joy of their mother's existence. While the mother lives, the child will be cared for; and the child knows this, instinctively, if not intelligently, and rejoices in knowing it. And to the children of God, as well, there is behind all that changes and can change the one unchangeable joy that God is. And while He is, His children will be cared for, and they ought to know it and rejoice in it, as instinctively and far more intelligently than the child of human parents. For what else can God do, being what He is? Neglect, indifference, forgetfulness, ignorance, are all impossible to Him. He knows everything, He cares about everything, He can manage everything, and He loves us! Surely this is enough for a "fullness of joy" beyond the power of words to express; no matter what else may be missed besides.

MOTHER IS THE HEART OF THE HOME, AND THE HOME IS THE HEART OF CHRISTMAS

Memories to treasure are made of Christmas Day—
Made of family gatherings and children as they play—
And always it is Mother who plays the leading part
In bringing joy and happiness to each expectant heart.
These memories grow more meaningful with every passing year—
More precious and more beautiful, more treasured and more dear—
And that is why at Christmastime there comes the happy thought
Of all the treasured memories that Mother's love has bought.
For no one gives more happiness or does more good for others
Than understanding, kind and wise and selfless, loving mothers.
And of all the loving mothers, the dearest one is you,
For you live Christmas every day in everything you do.

~HSR

The Desire to Give

He blesses the home of the righteous.
Proverbs 3:33 niv

I love to give my children things that they adore. I think that's why
I love Christmas shopping so much. I Christmas shop all year long.
If I see something that I know Abby or Allyson will adore, I'll buy
it and store it away for the holidays. However, I'm always tempted
to give those Christmas presents to the girls right away. In fact, a lot
of times, that's exactly what I do. I can't stand it. I just have to give
them their gifts early! I bet you do the same thing. We're moms. It's
our nature to give to our kids. We can't help ourselves!

As much as we love to give our kids the desires of their hearts, it
pales in comparison to how much our heavenly Father enjoys bless-
ing us. Where do you think that desire to give unto our children
comes from? God.

He is the best present-giver. He can hardly wait to give you that
new set of wing chairs that you've been longing for. He wants you to
have that Walt Disney World vacation. He loves to see us enjoying
the blessings He sends our way. So, enjoy your blessings today. By
doing that, you're blessing the Father.

Dear God,
I rejoice in Your presence and these precious moments alone with You.
Remain with me 24/7 as I share Your love with my little ones.
Show me ways to bring joy into their lives each and every day. Amen.

A MOTHER'S PRAYER

*I remember my mother's prayers
and they have always followed me.
They have clung to me all my life.*

ABRAHAM LINCOLN

"Your Father knows exactly what you need even before you ask him!"

Matthew 6:8 NLT

A MOTHER'S DAY PRAYER

Our Father in heaven, whose love is divine,
Thanks for the love of a mother like mine.
In Thy great mercy look down from above
And grant this dear mother the gift of Your love,
And all through the year, whatever betide her,
Assure her each day that You are beside her. . .
And, Father in heaven, show me the way
To lighten her tasks and brighten her day,
And bless her dear heart with the insight to see
That her love means more than the world to me.

~HSR

CIRCLES OF LOVE

Let us. . .love. . .with actions and in truth.
1 JOHN 3:18 NIV

One hot day last summer, my seventy-five-year-old mother, my eleven-year-old daughter, and I walked together across a sun-baked lawn. My mother's heart was bothering her, and we walked very slowly, but my daughter didn't mind; she's been complaining that I walk too fast ever since she was small. I listened to their soft voices, watching the way their heads bent toward each other, and I was startled to realize that my daughter is taller than my mother now. My mother said something, and I heard my daughter laugh out loud with delight.

And at that moment, I was suddenly, completely happy. I didn't want to be anywhere but right there, with the young woman to whom I had given life, with the older woman who had given me life. I thought of another woman, my mother's mother, now in heaven, and I imagined a young woman who is yet to be born, my daughter's daughter. Together we form a chain, a chain of love reaching from the past into the future.

An Easter Prayer for Mother

*This brings a loving Easter prayer that God will truly bless
Your Easter and the springtime with peace and happiness. . .
For, Mother, it has always been your faith in God above
That filled our home with happiness and our
hearts with truth and love.*

~HSR

God's Word in Their Hearts

*Trust in the LORD with all your heart and lean not on your own understanding;
in all your ways acknowledge him, and he will make your paths straight.*
PROVERBS 3:5–6 NIV

When I was eight years old in Vacation Bible School, I memorized
the above scripture. At the time, my motivation for learning this
important passage was a blue ribbon. Ahhh. . .the lure of a shiny blue
ribbon! Now, more than twenty years later, I've lost that ribbon, but
those words are still imprinted on my heart. They pop into my mind
at the times when I need them the most.

Today, as the mother of two little girls, I try to motivate my
children to memorize scripture, too. We recite them on the way to
school every morning, which has become a fun way to start the day.
Sometimes we try to see how fast we can say the verses. Other times,
we make up songs with them. With every recitation, we're putting
more of God's Word in our hearts.

As a mom, that's so comforting to me because I know that those
memory verses will pop into their minds whenever they need them
most. God's Word will be there for them even when I can't be—and
that's even better than a shiny blue ribbon!

Now I Lay Me
Down to Sleep

I remember so well this prayer I said
Each night as my mother tucked me in bed,
And today this same prayer is still the best way
To sign off with God at the end of the day
And to ask Him your soul to safely keep
As you wearily close your tired eyes in sleep,
Feeling content that the Father above
Will hold you secure in His great arms of love. . .
And having His promise that if ere you wake
His angels reach down, your sweet soul to take
Is perfect assurance that, awake or asleep,
God is always right there to tenderly keep
All of His children ever safe in His care,
For God's here and He's there and He's everywhere. . .
So into His hands each night as I sleep
I commend my soul for the dear Lord to keep,
Knowing that if my soul should take flight
It will soar to the land where there is no night.

~HSR

The Lord's Friendship

"I am the true vine, and My Father is the vinedresser. Abide in Me, and I in you. As the Father loved Me, I also have loved you; abide in My love."
John 15:1, 4, 9 NKJV

Here I am, Lord, after the late shift. Work was hard, fast, and stressful. I'm tired, but my body is so tense I can't sleep. All I can think of is the quiet peace You give me. Thank You, God, for meeting me here in my weariness and for Your friendship.

Your sweet presence fills the air. A feeling of expectancy greets me, as though You have been waiting for me to share my work events with You. I sense You listening intently to my every concern. The victories, the crises, even the funny happenings. I also bring my co-workers to You in prayer.

Like a new chapter in a book, I feel You speak to me. You comfort and assure me of answers to my prayers.

Thank You for my loved ones sleeping in nearby rooms. Their soft, steady breathing sounds so good. I ask Your blessings on each one and thank You for keeping them safe.

My eyelids grow heavy; I find it difficult to form my thoughts on You.

"Rest, my beloved," I feel You say.

Thank You, Lord, for meeting me here again and being my dearest Friend.

I Said a Prayer for You, Mother

I said a prayer for you, Mother,
I asked the Lord above
To keep you safely in His care
And enfold you in His love.
I did not ask for fortune,
For riches or for fame,
I only asked for blessings
In the Holy Savior's name—
Blessings to surround you
In times of trial and stress,
And inner joy to fill your heart
With peace and happiness.

~HSR

"God Bless Mommy"

And he said: "I tell you the truth, unless you change and become like little children, you will never enter the kingdom of heaven."
Matthew 18:3 niv

When Allyson was a preschooler, she loved to pray over our meals. She couldn't wait until that part of the day. I'd always ask, "Who wants to pray over our food?" Allyson would beam and shout, "ME! ME! ME!" And then she'd begin, "God bless Mommy, Daddy, Sister, Max (our dog), Ma-maw, Papaw, Nana, Granddad, Aunt Martie, Uncle Jan, Mandy, Autumn. . ." By the time Allyson finished her prayer, the food was totally cold. Still, there was something very sweet about her prayers. They were full of thanksgiving, humility, and genuineness.

I've learned a lot about prayer from my children. Both Abby and Allyson taught me to pray with enthusiasm, thanksgiving, and expectation. When Abby was only five, she prayed for her goldfish to live, and let me tell you, Bubbles was on his last fin. He was sort of swimming sideways in the bowl. He was fixing to go to the big fish bowl in the sky. But, Abby prayed and that little fish lived another two months. It was a miracle! She never had a doubt.

As moms, we need to have that same thankful heart and expectation when we pray to our heavenly Father. Learn from your little ones. They truly know how to pray.

At My Mother's Knee

I have worshiped in churches and chapels,
I have prayed in the busy street,
I have sought my God and found Him
Where the waves of the ocean beat.
I have knelt in a silent forest
In the shade of an ancient tree,
But the dearest of all my altars
Was raised at my mother's knee.
God, make me the woman of her vision
And purge me of all selfishness
And help keep me true to her standards
And help me to live and her to bless,
And then keep me a pilgrim forever
To the shrine at my mother's knee.

~HSR

A Constant Source

These older women must train the younger women
to love their husbands and their children.
TITUS 2:4 NLT

*I*t was my first night home from the hospital. Baby Abby was sleeping peacefully in my arms. She was so precious. But as I looked down into her little face, I panicked. I thought to myself, *I have no idea how to raise this little girl. I have a hard enough time just taking care of Jeff and myself and our dog!* I remember praying for God to send me help. That prayer was answered by way of my mother. She was (and still is) a constant source of encouragement, strength, wisdom, and laughter.

I've learned so much from my mother. Not only has she taught me about being a mom, but she's taught me how to be a better wife. When my father suffered three strokes over a year's time, I watched in amazement as my mother took care of Daddy. She was so strong and in control, yet so tender toward him. I thought, *Now that's the kind of wife I want to be.*

There is much to be learned from our elders, isn't there? That's why I love Titus 2:4 so much. Maybe your mom isn't a person you turn to for advice—and that's okay. God will send other wise women to be part of your life. Ask Him to do that for you today.

My dear loving and gracious Father,
Fill my children with Your love to overflowing. Send Your angels to guard
them. Allow my prayers for their health, hopes, and happiness to follow
them and cling to them now and forevermore, Amen.

A Mother's Hope

There are only two lasting bequests we can hope to give our children. One is roots; and the other, wings.

Hodding Carter

Point your kids in the right direction—
when they're old they won't be lost.

Proverbs 22:6 msg

MOTHERS WERE ONCE DAUGHTERS

Every home should have a daughter,
for there's nothing like a girl
To keep the world around her in one continuous whirl.
From the moment she arrives on earth
and on through womanhood,
A daughter is a female who is seldom understood.
One minute she is laughing, the next she starts to cry—
Man just can't understand her and there's just no use to try.
She is soft and sweet and cuddly but she's also wise and smart—
She's a wondrous combination of mind and brains and heart. . .
She starts out as a rosebud, with her beauty unrevealed,
Then through a happy childhood her petals are unsealed.
She's soon a sweet girl graduate and then a blushing bride
And then a lovely woman as the rosebud opens wide. . .
And someday in the future, if it be God's gracious will,
She, too, will be a mother and know that reverent thrill
That comes to every mother whose heart is filled with love
When she beholds the angel that God sent her from above. . .
And there would be no life at all in this world or the other
Without a darling daughter who in turn becomes a mother.

~HSR

HEARTS ENTWINED FOREVER

Above all, love each other deeply.
1 PETER 4:8 NIV

When my daughter Emily was little, she was my constant companion. Her little chattering voice brought new life to everything I did. Once, waiting in an examination room, the two of us were talking a blue streak when the nurse came in. "You two are best buddies, aren't you?" she said. And we were.

When Emily went to preschool, I gave her a gold heart of mine to wear, to remind her that my love went with her. When I went into the hospital for the birth of my second child, she gave it back to remind me that her love would be with me. And when she went to kindergarten, I bought her a duplicate necklace, so that she would know she was always in my heart.

But as she grew older and my life got busier, I sometimes worried that I would lose her, that she would disappear into her own new world of school and friends, and I would never recover the person who had been such a good companion to me.

As she becomes a young woman instead of a child, I find we relate to each other in a new way. Now, as we have woman-to-woman talks, I realize she's still a good companion. And yesterday, as she was hurrying off to meet her friends, I noticed the small gold heart that glittered at her throat. I touched the gold heart around my own neck and smiled.

LIFE'S FAIREST FLOWER

I have a garden within my soul of marvelous beauty rare,
Wherein the blossoms of all my life bloom ever in splendor fair.
Amid all this beauty and splendor,
one flower stands forth as queen
Alone in its great dazzling beauty, alone but ever supreme.
The flower of love and devotion has
guided me all through my life;
Softening my grief and my trouble,
sharing my toil and strife.
This flower has helped me conquer
temptation so black and grim,
And led me to victory and honor of my enemy, sin.
I have vainly sought in my garden thru
blossoms of love and light—
For a flower of equal wonder, to compare
with this one so bright.
But ever I met with failure, my search has been in vain—
For never a flower existed, like the blossom I can claim.
For after years I now can see, amid life's roses and rue—
God's greatest gift to a little child, my darling mother, was you.

~HSR

In the Garden

*Praise be to the God and Father of our Lord Jesus Christ,
the Father of compassion and the God of all comfort.*
2 Corinthians 1:3 NIV

Arla felt overwhelmed as she gazed at her mother's belongings. It had only been a few days since her mother passed away. Arla felt forsaken and lost. She sat wearily on a box in the garage and prayed for help through trembling lips. "I can't do this on my own, Lord," she whispered. . . .

She continued praying for a long time, the tears washing and cleansing her wounded heart. Finally, she stopped. A presence well known to Arla surrounded her: the comforting love of God.

Arla noticed the workbench. There lay her mother's gardening gloves and some small tools. Her mom often handed her a tool and showed how working the soil and flowers with her hands could be a good way of sorting out life's problems. Arla remembered them working alongside each other, sharing secrets and concerns, later taking them to God in prayer. God had touched her mom with a special gift of gardening and listening. . . .

She felt God's sweet comfort as she dug holes, planted bulbs, and dropped the seeds in place. Her thoughts cleared. Decisions Arla needed to make began falling into place. She knew she wasn't alone. She had the same wise, comforting God who had been with her mother and her all along.

A Gift of Life

A baby is a gift of life born of the wonder of love—
A little bit of eternity sent from the Father above,
Giving a new dimension to the love
between husband and wife
And putting an added new meaning to the
wonder and mystery of life.

~HSR

Our Newborn Baby

" 'The LORD bless you and keep you; the LORD make his face shine upon you and be gracious to you; the LORD turn his face toward you and give you peace.' "
NUMBERS 6:24–26 NIV

*L*ook at our beautiful baby, Lord, at these tiny fingers wrapped around mine. Look how this darling rests securely in my arms. See Daddy's proud gaze. Already my heart overflows with love. I talked to and prayed for this sweet one even while the baby was still in my womb.

Today, O Lord, I dedicate our baby as a love offering to You. Like Hannah in days of old, I thank You for giving our little one to us. Here and now, I present our child at Your altar to be raised for Your service.

Let Your angels encamp around and about us and protect us from evil and harm. Help us teach Your ways by truth and example. I pray that You will create a special hunger in this little heart to know, love, and serve You completely.

Help me remember our child is lent to us for a little while and that You are the lender. Let me not take our dear one back from You or pursue my own ways outside Your will.

I will bless Your name, O Lord, thanking You for this wonderful infant gift. I praise Your name in my thoughts, motives, and actions forever.

A Mother's Love Is Like a Haven
in the Storms of Life

A mother's love is like an island in life's ocean vast and wide—
A peaceful, quiet shelter from the restless, rising tide.
A mother's love is like a fortress, and we seek protection there
When the waves of tribulation seem to drown us in despair.
A mother's love is like a sanctuary where
our souls can find sweet rest
From the struggle and the tension of life's fast and futile quest.
A mother's love is like a tower rising far above the crowd,
And her smile is like the sun breaking
through a threatening cloud.
A mother's love is like a beacon burning bright
with faith and prayer,
And through the changing scenes of life we
can find a haven there.
For a mother's love is fashioned after God's enduring love—
It is endless and unfailing like the love of Him above.

~HSR

PROTECTING AT ALL COSTS

"Look at the birds of the air; they do not sow or reap or store away in barns, and yet your heavenly Father feeds them. Are you not much more valuable than they?"
MATTHEW 6:26 NIV

*M*ommy, hurry!" Abby called from the middle of the driveway. "It's a baby bird!"

Sure enough, right in the middle of our driveway was a sweet, fluffy, baby dove. He was probably five weeks old. He had all of his feathers, but the dainty dove still couldn't fly. After calling the Texas Wildlife Headquarters, I was instructed to move the bird into a make-shift nest in a hanging basket near the tree where he had fallen. As I planned my emergency bird rescue, I rushed to the front door to watch our little feathered friend. That's when I saw one of the most beautiful sights I'd ever seen—the mother dove nuzzling her baby bird—right in the middle of our driveway. She was protecting her baby at all costs.

We would do the same for our children. We'd give our life for our kids, wouldn't we? Do you know that's how God feels about us? He adores us! He cares about each one of us. When we fall out of our respective nests, He is right there, hovering over us, protecting us, loving us.

MOTHER'S DAY IS REMEMBRANCE DAY

Mother's Day is remembrance day,
and we pause on the path of the year
To pay honor and worshipful tribute
to the mothers our hearts hold dear.
For whether here or in heaven,
her love is our haven and guide,
For always the memory of Mother
is a beacon light shining inside.
Time cannot destroy her memory,
and years can never erase
The tenderness and the beauty of
the love in a mother's face.
And when we think of our mothers,
we draw nearer to God above,
For only God in His greatness
could fashion a mother's love.

~HSR

This Special Day

She watches over the affairs of her household and does not eat the bread of idleness.
Her children arise and call her blessed; her husband also, and he praises her.
PROVERBS 31:27–29 NIV

*L*ord, I collapse onto our couch, kick my shoes off, and think of today's blessings. Family and friends bustled around. Children chattered with youthful excitement. Steaming irresistible food simmered in the kitchen. Men exchanged stories and (thank You, Lord) helped with the little ones. It seems a whooshing dream; the day went so fast.

I reflect briefly on the struggles we've all had, the mountains we've fearfully conquered with Your help. Still we're together, loving and sharing. It was worth listening to each other and finding Your will through the years. I'm tired, but I loved it all. At nightfall, little arms wrapped around my neck with an "I love you, Nana." Strong embraces from sons so dear and tender hugs from loving daughters filled my heart with joy.

I thank You, Lord, for this day that You created and for the love of family and friends. As special days end in all their wild flurry, I'm often reminded of the true value in it all; not food, fancies, and elaborations, but my dearest friends and loved ones.

A CHILD'S FAITH

"*Jesus loves me, this I know,*
For the Bible tells me so."
Little children ask no more,
For love is all they're looking for,
And in a small child's shining eyes
The faith of all the ages lies.
And tiny hands and tousled heads
That kneel in prayer by little beds
Are closer to the dear Lord's heart
And of His kingdom more a part
Than we who search and never find
The answers to our questioning minds—
For faith in things we cannot see
Requires a child's simplicity.

~HSR

THROUGH LITTLE EYES

From the lips of children and infants you have ordained praise.
PSALM 8:2 NIV

*B*efore each child entered the crawl-around stage, I would crawl on all fours to "childproof" our home. As the girls have grown, I've realized that babyhood isn't the only time that it's important to look through a child's eyes.

Sometimes we moms are so busy that we forget our children have quite a lot to teach us—if we'll take the time to learn. Quite often what seems ordinary to us becomes spectacular from a child's perspective.

My friend Holly and her daughter were admiring a full moon when Mary Cate announced with three-year-old wonder, "Look, Mama, the moon has all its pieces!" With a smile and a hug, the moment was sealed in that mother's heart for all time.

Children remind us to laugh, no—giggle. They help us rediscover the simple joys of the sun on our face and grass under bare feet.

But even more important, children teach us about God. They show us how to pray believing and how to live abundantly. They take their heavenly Father at His Word, and they expect us to do the same.

What happiness God must feel when His little messengers reach the heart of an adult! For surely He is pleased when we remember to take joy in loving Him, in just being His child.

Dear Daddy God,
Renew my strength. Help me provide secure roots in which my little ones
may grow. Help me give them strong wings with which they may mount
up as eagles, soar over the rainbow, and alight in Your heavenly arms.
Amen.

A MOTHER'S BLESSING

*Maternal love: a miraculous substance
which God multiplies as He divides it.*
VICTOR HUGO

Discipline your son, and he will give you peace;
he will bring delight to your soul.

PROVERBS 29:17 NIV

The Greatest Career

*So glad a tiny baby came
To share your life and love and name,
For no doubt she is the greatest claim
That you have ever had to fame. . .
And don't misunderstand me, dear,
You were a star in your career,
But what, I ask you, is success
Compared with heaven's happiness?
And how could plaudits anywhere
Be half as wonderful and fair?
For this experience of the heart
Surpasses any skill or art,
For man excels in every line
But woman has a gift divine,
And in this world there is no other
As greatly honored as a mother.*

~HSR

LIVING TO GIVE

"Give, and it will be given to you: good measure,
pressed down, shaken together, and running over."
LUKE 6:38 NKJV

Did you know that God wants you to be happy? He desires for you to live life to its fullest. It doesn't matter that you might be elbow-deep in diapers and carpools right now—you can still enjoy life!

One of the main ways you can guarantee joy in your life is by living to give. You see, true happiness comes when we give of ourselves to others—our spouses, our children, our extended family, our church, our community, and our friends. As moms, we're sort of trained to be givers. We give up our careers, many times, to become full-time moms. We give up a full night's sleep to feed our babies. We give up sports cars for minivans and SUVs to accommodate our families. In fact, we'd give our lives for our children.

But sometimes our attitudes are less than joyful in all of our giving, right? Well, rejoice today. God promises to multiply back to you everything that you give. When you step out in faith, you open a door for God to move on your behalf. It's the simple principle of sowing and reaping. And as mothers, we are super sowers. So, get ready for a super huge harvest!

THE MAGIC OF LOVE

Love is like magic and it always will be,
For love still remains life's sweet mystery.
Love works in ways that are wondrous and strange,
And there's nothing in life that love cannot change.
Love can transform the most commonplace
Into beauty and splendor and sweetness and grace.
Love is unselfish, understanding, and kind,
For it sees with its heart and not with its mind.
Love gives and forgives—there is nothing too much
For love to heal with its magic touch.
Love is the language that every heart speaks,
For love is the one thing that every heart seeks. . .
And where there is love God, too, will abide
And bless the family residing inside.

~HSR

Embrace the Father's Love

"I have loved you with an everlasting love."
JEREMIAH 31:3 NIV

*L*ooking down into the face of my first newborn baby, I couldn't imagine loving anyone more than I loved her at that moment. She was everything I had dreamed of during those nine months of pregnancy. Jeff and I did all of the annoying baby talk and silly noises that all new parents do. We were absolutely captivated by her every sound, move, and facial expression. We adored her!

So, when I discovered I was pregnant with Baby Number Two on the eve before Abby's first birthday, I wondered, *Will I ever love another child as much as I love Abby?* I was worried. I just couldn't fathom loving another child as much as I loved "Baby Abbers," as we affectionately nicknamed her.

Then, Allyson Michelle Adams came into this world on August 15, 1994—bald and beautiful. I looked into her sweet face and fell in love all over again. Jeff and I discovered that we could love another baby just as much as our first. We always tell our girls, "You are *both* our favorites!" Do you know that is exactly how God sees us? He doesn't love you or me more than anyone else—we're all His favorites! Meditate on that today and embrace the Father's love.

OUR MOTHER

Who has an understanding way?
A faith that nothing can dismay?
Who loves us dearly, come what may?
Our mother!
Who helps us laugh away our fears?
Who heals our hurts and dries our tears?
Who holds us closely through the years?
Our mother!
Whom do we honor with our love?
Who is a gift from heaven above?
Whom do we think the whole world of?
Our mother!

~HSR

UNDERSTANDING

"To God belong wisdom and power; counsel and understanding are his."
JOB 12:13 NIV

*Y*ou are ruining my life!"

That's what the daughter screamed at her mother in the recent remake of Disney's *Freaky Friday*. We took the girls to see that movie earlier this month, and all of us enjoyed it—especially me. I could totally relate to the mother in the film. I, too, am a member of the "You've ruined my life!" club. Abby has told me that more than once.

You know, on days when your beloved child looks you in the face and says, "You're ruining my life," you don't want to be nice. Actually, you want to be defensive. You want to say, "Listen, kiddo, do you have any idea what I do for you every single day? You couldn't make it without me!" (And yes, I have said those things.)

But, what the mother discovers in *Freaky Friday* is that she lacks understanding where her daughter is concerned and vice versa. Once the mom and daughter see things through the other's eyes, understanding comes. If you're also a member of the "You've ruined my life" club, ask God to give you understanding so that you can see things through your kids' eyes. If you do, I have a feeling your membership in that club will soon expire.

God Made Loving Mothers

God made the sun, He made the sky.
He made the trees and the birds that fly.
God made the flowers, He made the light,
He made the stars that shine at night.
God made the rain, He made the dew,
And He made loving mothers, too—
Dear and special ones like you.

~HSR

GOD'S WORKMANSHIP

For we are God's workmanship, created in Christ Jesus to do good works,
which God prepared in advance for us to do.
EPHESIANS 2:10 NIV

I've always loved this scripture. Did you know that the word *workmanship* indicates an ongoing process? So, if we are God's workmanship, we are God's ongoing project. In other words, He isn't finished with us yet! Isn't that good news? I am so glad! I'd hate to think that I was as good as I was going to get.

So, if you are feeling less than adequate today, thinking that you are a terrible mother and wife and Christian—cheer up! God is not through with you yet! In fact, He is working on you right now—even as you're reading this devotional. He knew that we'd all make big mistakes, but this scripture says that He created us in Christ Jesus to do good works. He's prepared the road for us. He's been planning our steps long before we arrived here, so don't worry!

We may not be where we want to be today, but as long as we're further along than we were yesterday, we're making progress. We're on the right road. After all, we're God's workmanship, and He only turns out good stuff!

ON MOTHER'S DAY MY THOUGHTS GO BACK

On Mother's Day my thoughts go back
To all the years that have gone before,
And all of my love and good wishes
Go straight to that open door.
For always the door to your heart and home
Stood open with welcoming cheer,
And memories of you
Grow dearer each year.

~HSR

Making Memories

"Love one another, even as I have loved you."
John 13:34 nasb

When was the last time you slowed down long enough to make mud pies with your kids? When was the last time you read funny poetry by a candlelight pizza dinner? If it's been awhile, then plan a special day to do nothing but fun stuff with your children. Of course, this works much better if your kids are willing to spend an entire day with you. Once they reach puberty, Mom is sort of on the "nerd list." But, if you still have little ones or tweens running around, why not host an all-out fun-filled day?

Begin with pizza for breakfast. Watch funny, family films in your jammies until noon. Then, if the weather is nice, take a bike ride together or go on a scavenger hunt in a nearby park. Play board games until nightfall. Finish the day with devotions and prayer time. Just bask in each other's presence, soaking it all in.

At the end of the day, you will have made some magnificent memories. When your kids are old, they'll look back on that day and smile. They may not remember exactly what you did, but they'll remember the love.

MOTHERS NEVER DIE,
THEY JUST KEEP HOUSE UP IN THE SKY

When we are children, we are happy each day
And our mother is young, and she laughs as we play.
Then as we grow up, she teaches us truth
And lays life's foundation in the days of our youth.
Then it's time for us to leave home,
But her teachings go with us wherever we roam. . .
As she grows older, we look back with love,
Knowing that mothers are gifts from above.
And when she goes home to receive her reward,
She will dwell in God's kingdom and keep house for the Lord
Where she'll light up the stars that shine through the night
And keep all the moonbeams sparkling and bright,
And then with the dawn, she'll put darkness away
As she scours the sun to new brilliance each day.
So dry tears of sorrow, for mothers don't die—
They just move in with God and keep house in the sky,
And there in God's kingdom mothers watch from above
To welcome their children with their undying love.

~HSR

By This I Know

I am the resurrection, and the life: he that believeth in me, though he were dead, yet shall he live: and whosoever liveth and believeth in me shall never die.
JOHN 11:25–26 KJV

What will it be like when Jesus takes us to heaven and says, "See, here is your loved one, perfect, and whole, and like Me!" We will be reunited in fully satisfying, never-ending joy!

Then we will know with surety, without doubt, and forever that the Word of God is true! But we can trust God's Word now, even in death. He has promised. Do you believe Him?

The promise is certain for each individual—from the beginning of time until the end of it—who believes in the Lord Jesus Christ for forgiveness of sin. The house of clay, that vehicle God has provided us for living on earth, doing His will, and glorifying His name, may wear out and die. It will be left below for now. But soul and spirit will live—immediately at leaving the body and forever—in God's presence. Even the body will be resurrected and changed to fitness for life in eternity. First Corinthians 15 tells that it will be changed to be like Jesus' glorified body. Body, soul, and spirit will be reunited when Jesus comes in the Rapture to call all believers to be with Him eternally.

God alone holds the breath of life.

A MOTHER'S LOVE
CAN NEVER DIE

Your mother is still with you—she never left your side.
She still is close about you—her spirit is your guide,
For the blessed memory of her will lead you through each day,
And the tender thoughts you have of
her are in your heart to stay.

~HSR

Carrying on the Tradition

They were also to stand every morning to thank and praise the LORD.
1 Chronicles 23:30 NIV

I've never been much of a morning person. This was especially true when I was a child. I'd wait until the absolute last possible moment to get out of bed. But, my morning "wake-up call" began at 6 a.m. every weekday, courtesy of my mother, Marion, who *is* a morning person.

She didn't just knock on the door and say "Time to get up." Oh, no—she was far too joyful for that. My mother had an entire musical extravaganza worked out. She'd begin with her rendition of "This is the day that the Lord has made. We will rejoice and be glad in it." All of this singing was accompanied by very loud handclapping, and if that didn't do the trick, she would flip the lights on and off in time to her singing.

As you might have guessed, I proudly carry on this tradition. I even sing the same song, accompanied by loud handclaps and my own light show. And my kids moan and groan, much the same way I did. Nevertheless, we begin each day praising God and thanking Him for another day—some of us a little more than others! We're starting the day on the right note—why not join in the fun?

WHERE DOES THE TIME GO?

Where does the time go in its endless flight?
Spring turns to fall and day to night,
And little girls grow up and marry,
For years fly by and do not tarry.
And though it seems like yesterday
That she was busily at play,
The months and years have quickly flown
And your small doll is now full-grown.

~HSR

Growing Up, Letting Go

*"Build up, build up, prepare the road!
Remove the obstacles out of the way of my people."*
Isaiah 57:14 niv

I can do it by myself!"

"I know you can, honey, but Mommy just wants to help you."

"I don't need your help!"

I've dreamed of this moment for years—the time when the girls would actually start doing more for themselves. But now something just does not feel quite right.

This vague feeling of loss is a continuous process. From their infancy until the present, our children's level of dependency on Roy and me has changed dramatically.

As parents, we knew this would happen. In fact, we prayed that our children would grow up to be strong, independent adults. But it still isn't easy to let go.

I'll never forget Laura's first day of school. My legs were like lead as I left her in a classroom of near strangers. My vision was cloudy with tears, and I knew I had to get out of there fast before everyone saw Laura's mommy cry like a baby.

Of course when Mary starts "big school," I'll experience it all over again, but that's all right. All these little "letting go's" are preparing me for the big ones later on. And I know that when the day arrives and the girls walk away into college, marriage, or a career, I'll feel pretty much the same way. And I'll breathe pretty much the same prayer, "Oh God, how I love these girls. . .please take care of them for us!"

BLESSED ABUNDANTLY

*Love alone can make us kind
And give us joy and peace of mind,
So live with joy unselfishly
And you'll be blessed abundantly.*

~HSR

Refueled with His Love

But Jesus Himself would often slip away to the wilderness and pray.
Luke 5:16 nasb

Retreat and replenish." Remember that phrase? It's helped me a lot over the past few years. Every time I feel I have nothing left to give, Jesus reminds me that it's time to retreat and replenish. By spending time on my knees and in His Word, I am refilled with God's love, power, strength, joy, and energy. I give God all of my worries, sickness, concerns, tiredness, and grouchiness, and He gives me all the good stuff. What a deal, eh? Even Jesus recognized the need to retreat and replenish. After He had healed many people and driven out demons, He needed to retreat and replenish, too.

If you're feeling worn out today, turn to God. Let Him reenergize you. Let Him refuel you with His love so that you'll have love to give your children. As moms, we have to refuel so that we are ready to minister to our families.

As moms, we set the tone for the home. If we're stressed out and drained, our homes will be full of stress and confusion. So, do yourself and your family a favor and retreat and replenish. God is ready to fill you up!

TREASURES

Give Him a chance to open His treasures,
And He'll fill your life with unfathomable pleasures—
Pleasures that never grow worn out and faded
And leave us depleted, disillusioned, and jaded—
For God has a storehouse just filled to the brim
With all that man needs, if we'll only ask Him.

~HSR

ABOVE ALL THAT WE COULD EVER ASK

Now to Him who is able to do far more abundantly beyond all that we ask or think,
according to the power that works within us.
EPHESIANS 3:20 NASB

When I was a little girl growing up in Indiana, I was the classic daydreamer. I'd sit in class, look out the window, and dream of being anywhere but in Mrs. Webster's room. I couldn't wait to grow up and have a life that didn't include homework. Now that I'm all grown up, I still daydream. I've traded homework for housework, but basically I feel like that same little girl on the inside.

I still have hopes and dreams that I think about on a daily basis. I still believe that God is going to do big things for me. And now, twenty-five years since I was in Mrs. Webster's fourth-grade class, I know that God is capable of doing the impossible in my life. He has proven Himself to me time and time again.

Has God proven Himself to you? Do you have confidence that He is able to do above all that we could ever ask or think? Now, I don't know about you, but I can ask and think of a lot of stuff, so that verse totally excites me. It should totally excite you, too. If you've never seen the power of God in your life, ask Him to show Himself strong to you today. He will. He's just been waiting for you to ask.

Dear Heavenly Father,
Thank You for allowing me to experience the precious gift of
motherhood and for giving me the opportunity to raise a child
in this world. Please allow me to reflect Your love so
my children can see You in me. Amen.

*B*orn in 1900 in Ohio, **Helen Steiner Rice** began writing at an early age. In 1918, Helen took a job at a public utilities company, eventually becoming one of the first female advertising managers and public speakers in the country. At age twenty-nine, she married banker Franklin Rice, who committed suicide in 1932, never having fully recovered mentally and financially from losses incurred during the Great Depression.

Following her husband's death, Helen used her gift of verse to encourage others. Her talents came to the attention of the nation when her greeting card poem "The Priceless Gift of Christmas" was read on the *Lawrence Welk Show*. Soon a series of poetry books, a source of inspiration to people worldwide, followed. Helen died in 1981, leaving a foundation that offers assistance to the needy and elderly.

Scripture Index

Old Testament

New Testament